EXPLORING THE STATES
Hawaii
THE ALOHA STATE

by Emily Rose Oachs

BLASTOFF!
5
READERS

BELLWETHER MEDIA • MINNEAPOLIS, MN

Note to Librarians, Teachers, and Parents:

Blastoff! Readers are carefully developed by literacy experts and combine standards-based content with developmentally appropriate text.

Level 1 provides the most support through repetition of high-frequency words, light text, predictable sentence patterns, and strong visual support.

Level 2 offers early readers a bit more challenge through varied simple sentences, increased text load, and less repetition of high-frequency words.

Level 3 advances early-fluent readers toward fluency through increased text and concept load, less reliance on visuals, longer sentences, and more literary language.

Level 4 builds reading stamina by providing more text per page, increased use of punctuation, greater variation in sentence patterns, and increasingly challenging vocabulary.

Level 5 encourages children to move from "learning to read" to "reading to learn" by providing even more text, varied writing styles, and less familiar topics.

Whichever book is right for your reader, Blastoff! Readers are the perfect books to build confidence and encourage a love of reading that will last a lifetime!

This edition first published in 2014 by Bellwether Media, Inc.

No part of this publication may be reproduced in whole or in part without written permission of the publisher. For information regarding permission, write to Bellwether Media, Inc., Attention: Permissions Department, 5357 Penn Avenue South, Minneapolis, MN 55419.

Library of Congress Cataloging-in-Publication Data

Oachs, Emily Rose.
 Hawaii / by Emily Rose Oachs.
    pages cm. – (Blastoff! readers. Exploring the states)
 Includes bibliographical references and index.
 Summary: "Developed by literacy experts for students in grades three through seven, this book introduces young readers to the geography and culture of Hawaii"– Provided by publisher.
 ISBN 978-1-62617-010-0 (hardcover : alk. paper)
 1. Hawaii–Juvenile literature. I. Title.
 DU623.25.O23 2013
 996.9–dc23
                                                        2013002386

Printed in the United States of America, North Mankato, MN.

Table of Contents

Where Is Hawaii?

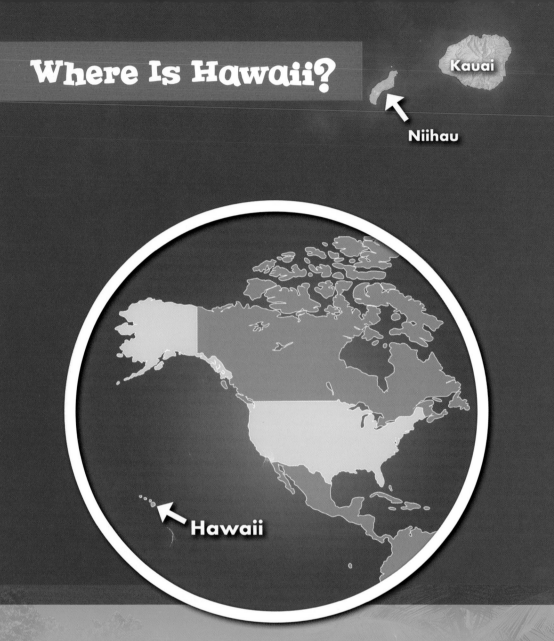

Kauai

Niihau

Hawaii

The state of Hawaii is an **archipelago** in the Pacific Ocean. It lies about 2,400 miles (3,860 kilometers) southwest of the United States **mainland**. Hawaii is the only island state. It is also the southernmost state. It extends as far south as southern Mexico.

Pacific Ocean

N

W   E

S

Oahu

Honolulu

Molokai

Lanai

Maui

Kahoolawe

Hilo

Hawaii

Did you know?
Hawaii's islets are too small for humans to live on.

Hawaii Volcanoes
National Park

Hawaii is a string of 132 islands. Together they cover 6,468 square miles (16,752 square kilometers) of land. The eight main islands are Hawaii, Maui, Kahoolawe, Lanai, Molokai, Oahu, Kauai, and Niihau. The other 124 **islets** cover only about 3 square miles (8 square kilometers) in total. Honolulu is the state capital. It is located on the island of Oahu.

History

Hawaii's first settlers were Polynesians. They sailed to the islands in **outrigger canoes**. King Kamehameha I united the Hawaiian Islands by 1810. He became Hawaii's first **monarch**. In 1898, the United States took control of Hawaii. The Japanese military attacked Oahu's Pearl Harbor on December 7, 1941. In 1959, Hawaii became the fiftieth state.

King
Kamehameha I

Did you know?
Hawaii is the only state that is a former royal kingdom.

Hawaii Timeline!

300-700: The first Polynesians arrive from the Marquesas Islands.

800-1200: A second group of Polynesians travels to Hawaii from Tahiti.

1778: Captain James Cook becomes the first known European to reach Hawaii.

1810: All the Hawaiian Islands are united under King Kamehameha I's rule.

1893: Queen Liliuokalani, Hawaii's last monarch, is forced out of power.

1898: The United States takes control of Hawaii.

1941: Japanese forces bomb Pearl Harbor, a military base on Oahu.

1959: Hawaii becomes the fiftieth state on August 21.

2008: Hawaii native Barack Obama is elected the forty-fourth President of the United States.

Queen Liliuokalani

Attack on Pearl Harbor

Barack Obama

The Land

Hawaii's 132 islands form a curve that extends 1,500 miles (2,400 kilometers). The 124 islets are made of either rock or **coral** and sand. The eight main islands feature many landforms. Canyons carve the landscape of several. Majestic, deeply grooved cliffs rise along Kauai's Na Pali Coast. Snowcapped mountains tower over sandy beaches on the island of Hawaii. Throughout the state, rivers and streams carry water from the mountains to the ocean. Beautiful waterfalls spill down mountainsides.

Trade winds from the northeast contribute to Hawaii's mild **tropical** climate. **Rain forests** cover parts of the state that receive a lot of rainfall. Other parts are dry.

fun fact

Kauai's Mount Waialeale receives about 460 inches (1,170 centimeters) of rain each year. It is the wettest place on the planet!

Mount Waialeale

Na Pali Coast
Kauai

Hawaii's Climate
average °F

spring
Low: 67°
High: 81°

summer
Low: 72°
High: 85°

fall
Low: 71°
High: 85°

winter
Low: 66°
High: 80°

Did you know?
Hawaiian beaches come in many colors. Rocks have broken down into black, green, and red sands. Powerful waves break shells and coral into white sands.

Volcanoes

Hawaii Volcanoes National Park

Did you know?
Hawaii Volcanoes National Park and Haleakala National Park allow visitors to get a closer view of active and dormant volcanoes.

Underwater **volcanoes** created the Hawaiian Islands millions of years ago. When volcanoes erupt, their **lava** hardens as it hits cool water. Over time, the volcanoes build up to the ocean's surface to form islands.

Most of Hawaii's volcanoes are **dormant**. Only three active volcanoes remain in the state. Kilauea and Mauna Loa are both on the island of Hawaii. Mauna Loa is the world's largest volcano. It rises to 13,677 feet (4,169 meters). Loihi is an underwater volcano southeast of the island of Hawaii. Scientists do not know when Loihi will break the ocean's surface. They believe it may become Hawaii's ninth major island in 10,000 to 250,000 years.

fun fact

Kilauea is one of the world's most active volcanoes. It has been erupting continuously since 1983.

Kilauea

Wildlife

Some of Hawaii's animals are unlike any others on the planet. They have **evolved** far away from other wildlife. The Hawaiian hoary bat is the state's only **native** land mammal. Native birds are more plentiful. More than 40 kinds of Hawaiian honeycreepers live in the forests. Every year, the golden plover flies more than 3,000 miles (4,800 kilometers) from Alaska to spend winter in Hawaii.

Humpback whales travel to Hawaii each year to mate and give birth. Hawaiian monk seals nurse their pups on the island's beaches. Viper dogfish lurk in the Pacific waters where bottlenose dolphins swim. Sea turtles find shelter in the **coral reefs**.

golden plover

humpback whale

sea turtle

Hawaiian monk seal

13

Landmarks

Plenty of historical and cultural sites stand among Hawaii's natural beauty. The Hawaiian monarchs once lived in Iolani Palace in Honolulu. It is the only royal palace in the United States. The Honolulu Museum of Art is celebrated for its collection of Asian art. The museum also houses works by Claude Monet and Pablo Picasso.

The USS *Arizona* Memorial stands in Pearl Harbor over the wreckage of the sunken ship. The memorial was built to remember the people killed in the Pearl Harbor attack. On Molokai, the historic Kapuaiwa Coconut Grove contains 1,000 trees. King Kamehameha V had them planted in 1863. A nearby sign warns of falling coconuts.

USS Arizona Memorial

fun fact

King Kamehameha V had a coconut tree planted for each of his warriors. The trees also shaded the royal bathing pools.

Kapuaiwa Coconut Grove

Iolani Palace

Honolulu

Waikiki Beach

Honolulu is located on the southeastern shore of Oahu. Its name is Hawaiian for "sheltered bay." It is built on a harbor protected by a reef and an island. Punchbowl Crater stands near the center of Honolulu. It was formed by a volcano. Now the crater is home to the National Memorial Cemetery of the Pacific.

About three out of every four Hawaiians live in the
Honolulu area. The city was once an important location
for sandalwood traders and whale hunters. It continues
to be Hawaii's main **port**. Today, millions of **tourists**
visit Honolulu each year. Most of them stay near Waikiki
Beach, a popular surfing spot.

Working

Did you know?
Hawaii is one of the world's largest producers of macadamia nuts.

Most Hawaiians have **service jobs**. Some are hired by the government to work in schools and hospitals. Many serve the state's tourists at restaurants, resorts, golf courses, and shops. Hawaiians also work for the U.S. military. The Air Force, Navy, Marines, and Army all have bases in the state.

Small Hawaiian farms grow fresh vegetables for locals to eat. Larger farms produce sugarcane, pineapples, and coffee beans. Some farmers raise tropical flowers, such as orchids, to **export**. Others keep cattle ranches. Off the coast, fishers catch tuna and swordfish. Factory workers in Honolulu produce sugar, bread, and other food products.

Where People Work in Hawaii

manufacturing
2%

farming and
natural resources
2%

government
21%

services
75%

Playing

Hawaii provides land and water for all kinds of outdoor adventures. The clear ocean waters off the coasts are perfect for snorkeling, scuba diving, and whale watching. Windsurfers compete off Oahu's coast. The peaks of Mauna Loa and Mauna Kea are so high that they receive snowfall. In winter, people ski down their slopes!

Surfing is a popular Hawaiian sport. It was invented by ancient Polynesians. In the early 1900s, the sport spread from Hawaii across the globe. Each year, the world's most talented surfers gather to compete at the Vans Triple Crown of Surfing on Oahu's North Shore.

fun fact

Oahu hosted the first Ironman Triathlon in 1978. Racers had to swim 2.4 miles (3.9 kilometers) in the ocean, bicycle 112 miles (180 kilometers) around Oahu, and then run 26.2 miles (42 kilometers) through Honolulu.

Vans Triple Crown of Surfing

Haupia

Ingredients:

2 cups coconut milk

1 cup whole milk

6 tablespoons sugar

5 tablespoons cornstarch

1/4 teaspoon vanilla

Directions:

1. Pour one cup of coconut milk into a saucepan. Combine sugar and cornstarch and stir into coconut milk.

2. Add vanilla. Stir over low heat until thickened.

3. Add remainder of coconut milk and whole milk and continue to heat until thickened.

4. Pour into 8-inch square pan and chill until firm.

Note:

Haupia is thicker than regular pudding. Cut into small squares and serve on *ti* leaves.

kalua pig

poi

Hawaiians have an abundance of fresh food to eat. Pineapples and mangoes ripen in the sun. Coconuts drop onto the beaches from trees. The ocean provides fish such as *mahi mahi* and *opakapaka*.

In Hawaii, people often gather for feasts called luaus. At a luau, a whole pig is cooked in an underground pit to make *kalua* pig. Another popular luau dish is *poi*. To prepare *poi*, the root of a taro plant is pounded into a paste. *Lomi lomi* salmon is a **traditional** salad made of salmon and tomatoes. A coconut dish called *haupia* is served for dessert.

23

Festivals

Every January, Hawaiians observe the Chinese New Year with food, crafts, and traditional Chinese lion dancers. The Japanese *Bon* Festival takes place from June until August on each of the islands. Every weekend, Hawaiians gather for *bon* dances to honor their **ancestors**.

In September, the Aloha Festivals bring locals and visitors together to celebrate Hawaii's heritage. The festivals occur on most of the islands and feature feasts, parades, and dancing. The Hawaii International Film Festival takes place across the state in October. People come from around the world to see films from more than 45 countries.

fun fact

Bon comes from the Japanese word *O-bon*. It means "lantern festival." People believe the lanterns that light the festival lead their ancestors' spirits back to visit.

Bon Festival

Aloha Festival

Aloha FESTIVAL

The hula is a traditional Hawaiian dance. For centuries, early Hawaiians did not have a written language. They danced the hula to tell stories of their history and culture. Now hula dancing is a highlight at most Hawaiian festivals and luaus.

Hula dancers wear **leis** around their heads, ankles, wrists, and necks. They sway their hips and move their hands to the rhythm of a chant or song. The hula is just one part of Hawaii's rich culture. This graceful dance reflects the beauty of the Hawaiian Islands.

Did you know?
The Merrie Monarch Festival in Hilo celebrates Hawaiian culture. It features dance performances and a hula competition.

Fast Facts About Hawaii

Hawaii's Flag

The Hawaiian flag has eight horizontal stripes of white, red, and blue. The British flag is in the upper left corner. King Kamehameha I received the British flag as a gift and used it as Hawaii's flag. The eight stripes were later added to represent the eight main islands of Hawaii.

State Flower
hibiscus

State Nickname:	The Aloha State
State Motto:	"The Life of the Land is Perpetuated in Righteousness"
Year of Statehood:	1959
Capital City:	Honolulu
Other Major Cities:	Hilo, Kailua, Kaneohe
Population:	1,360,301 (2010)
Area:	6,468 square miles (16,752 square kilometers); Hawaii is the 43rd largest state.
Major Industries:	military, tourism, farming
Natural Resources:	soil, plants, water
State Government:	51 representatives; 25 senators
Federal Government:	2 representatives; 2 senators
Electoral Votes:	4

State Bird
Hawaiian goose

State Animal
Hawaiian monk seal

Glossary

ancestors—relatives who lived long ago

archipelago—a chain of islands

coral—small ocean animals whose skeletons make up coral reefs

coral reefs—structures made of coral that usually grow in shallow seawater

dormant—no longer active

evolved—gradually changed or developed

export—to sell to another country

islets—small islands

lava—hot, melted rock that flows out of an active volcano

leis—wreaths that are usually made of flowers or leaves; leis can also be made with coral, feathers, or shells.

mainland—the main body of a country

monarch—a country's ruler; kings and queens are monarchs.

native—originally from a specific place

outrigger canoes—canoes with floating supports that extend out from the boat; ancient Polynesians used outrigger canoes to sail to Hawaii.

port—a sea harbor where ships can dock

rain forests—thick, green forests that are found in the hot and wet regions near the equator

service jobs—jobs that perform tasks for people or businesses

tourists—people who travel to visit another place

trade winds—winds that blow constantly and from only one direction

traditional—relating to a custom, idea, or belief handed down from one generation to the next

tropical—part of the tropics; the tropics is a hot, rainy region near the equator.

volcanoes—holes in the earth; when a volcano erupts, hot, melted rock called lava shoots out.

To Learn More

AT THE LIBRARY

Benoit, Peter. *The Attack on Pearl Harbor*. New York, N.Y.: Children's Press, 2013.

Mattern, Joanne. *Hawaii: Past and Present*. New York, N.Y.: Rosen Central, 2011.

Miller, Debbie S. *Flight of the Golden Plover: The Amazing Migration Between Hawaii and Alaska*. Fairbanks, Alaska: University of Alaska Press, 2011.

ON THE WEB

Learning more about Hawaii is as easy as 1, 2, 3.

1. Go to www.factsurfer.com.

2. Enter "Hawaii" into the search box.

3. Click the "Surf" button and you will see a list of related Web sites.

With factsurfer.com, finding more information is just a click away.

Index

The images in this book are reproduced through the courtesy of: Vibrant Images Studio, front cover (bottom); Guynamedjames, p. 6; (Collection)/ Prints & Photographs Division/ Library of Congress, p. 7 (left, middle, right); Caleb Foster, p. 8; Fremme, pp. 8-9; Col, pp. 10-11; Douglas Peebles/ Glow Images, p. 11; Idreamphoto, p. 12 (left); David Ashley, p. 12 (middle); Arnold van Wijk, p. 12 (right); David Fleetham/ Visuals Unlimited, Inc./ Getty Images, pp. 12-13; Chromorange/ picture-alliance/ Newscom, p. 14 (bottom); Pingger, p. 14 (top); Maridav, pp. 14-15; Lorcell, pp. 16-17; David R. Frazier/ DanitaDelimont.com "Danita Delimont Photography"/ Newscom, p. 18; Lonely Planet Images/ Getty Images, p. 19; Elizabeth Kreutz/ Zuma Press/ Newscom, p. 20; Kelly Cestari/ Zuma Press/ Newscom, pp. 20-21; Nancy Nehring, p. 22; Chris Cheadle/ All Canada Photos/ SuperStock, p. 23; Design Pics/ Tomas del Amo/ Newscom, p. 23 (right); Bon Dance, Honolulu, Oahu, Hawaii/ SuperStock, p. 24; Associated Press, pp. 24-25; Boykov, pp. 26-27; Pakmor, p. 28 (top); Fotofermer, p. 28 (bottom); Radoslaw Lecyk, p. 29 (left); Masa Ushioda/ Age Fotostock/ SuperStock, p. 29 (right).